CELEBRATING THE PEOPLES AND CIVILIZATIONS OF AFRICA

THE
MAASAI
OF EAST AFRICA

Jamie Hetfield

The Rosen Publishing Group's

New York

Published in 1996 by The Rosen Publishing Group, Inc.
29 East 21st Street, New York, NY 10010

First Edition

Photo credits: Cover © CFM, Nairobi; p. 4 © Buddy Mays/International Stock; pp. 7, 15 © G. E. Pakenham/International Stock; pp. 8, 16 © Wendy Stone/Gamma Liaison; pp. 11, 12 © David Cimino/International Stock; p. 19 © Seena Sussman/International Stock; p. 20 © Chad Ehlers/International Stock.

Book design and layout: Kim Sonsky

Hetfield, Jamie.
    Maasai / Jamie Hetfield
          p.   cm. — (Celebrating the peoples and civilizations of Africa)
    Includes index.
    Summary: Describes the customs, traditions, food, clothes, and homes of the Maasai people, who live in the grasslands of eastern Africa.
    ISBN 0-8239-2330-4
    1. Masai (African people)—Social life and customs—Juvenile literature.   [1. Masai (African people) 2. Africa, East—Social life and customs.] I. Title. II. Series.
    DT433.545.M33H64 1996
    306' .089' 965—dc20   95-51762
                                          CIP
                                          AC

Manufactured in the United States of America

CONTENTS

THE MAASAI OF EASTERN AFRICA

The **Maasai** (MAH-sigh) live in one of the most beautiful places in the world, the **savannas** (sa-VAN-nuz) of eastern Africa. These are grasslands that stretch as far as you can see. The Maasai call their land Maasailand.

In the eastern part of Maasailand, rolling green hills lead to **Mt. Kilimanjaro** (mount kil-i-mon-JA-roe). It is the highest mountain in all of Africa. Snow covers its top for most of the year.

Wild animals like lions, zebras, elephants, and antelope also share this beautiful land.

◄ Maasailand stretches across the savannas of eastern Africa.

HOW THE MAASAI LIVE

The Maasai are a strong, proud people. Their warriors are known for their great strength and courage.

The Maasai are herders who raise cattle. They do not keep their cattle behind fences. Instead, the cattle roam across the savanna in search of fresh grass and water. The Maasai roam with them to take care of them. The Maasai survive by getting milk, food, and leather from cattle.

The Maasai roam with their ▶ cattle across the savanna.

A MAASAI HOME

When a group of Maasai move to a new place, they build a small village. It is called an **engang** (n-GANG).

First, the men build a tall fence made of thornbushes in the shape of a huge circle. The prickly branches of the thornbushes help protect them from **predators** (PRE-da-torz) and cattle thieves.

Then, inside the fence, the women build small houses out of grass and a mixture of mud. In the center of the *engang* is a big open area for the cattle to stay in at night.

◄ Maasai women build the houses that their families live in.

A MAASAI MEAL

The main part of the Maasai's diet is milk, which they get from their cows. They also drink the blood of their cattle. Warriors drink the blood to make them stronger. A woman who has just had a baby drinks the blood to help her get her strength back. They also eat potatoes, bread, and sugar, which they buy from stores in nearby towns.

Maasai do eat the meat of their cattle, but only during special ceremonies.

The Maasai believe that drinking a cow's blood helps a new mother regain her strength. ▶

MAASAI CLOTHING

The Maasai wear long cotton cloths called *lubegas* (loo-BAY-gas). These colorful clothes are usually red, brown, or orange. Some have bold stripes and fancy designs.

All Maasai wear beautiful necklaces and earrings made of blue, orange, and red beads. Sometimes they wear so many necklaces that you can't even see their necks!

The Maasai sometimes paint beautiful triangles, stripes, and swirls on their bodies with a mixture of earth and a red or white mineral called **ocher** (OH-kur).

◀ Both Maasai men and women wear beautiful clothes and jewelry.

MAASAI CHILDREN

Both girls and boys learn how to take care of their family's herds by taking care of the young animals.

Children are taught to sing to the cattle. Each cow has its own personality. Children learn how to tell them apart by learning the shape of each animal's horns and the different colors of their hides.

Maasai children also spend a lot of time playing. One of their favorite games is hide-and-seek!

Maasai children learn how to raise cattle by working as shepherds. ▶

BECOMING A WOMAN

Among the Maasai, one of the most important days of a girl's life is her wedding day. The bride and her family shave their heads and paint them with red ocher. They dress in soft leather hides and wear their most beautiful necklaces.

Then the groom slowly leads the bride and her family to his house. When she gets to her new home, the bride is given many gifts of milk, meat, and honey.

Everyone celebrates this wonderful day by singing and dancing.

◀ A bride's mother drips milk on the bride's feet as part of the wedding ceremony.

BECOMING A MAN

A Maasai boy becomes a young warrior when he is about 14 years old. A few years later, as a test of manhood, he goes into the wild alone. There he hopes to kill a lion. If he does this, he proudly wears the **mane** (MAIN) of the lion as a headdress.

Warriors also have jumping contests. They jump high up in the air, like jumping on pogo sticks.

Warriors are fearless protectors of their people. They are brave and smart, but they are also gentle.

Maasai warriors are famous for jumping high off the ground in special dances. ▶

KENYA AND TANZANIA

The Maasai live in the countries of **Kenya** (KEN-ya) and **Tanzania** (tan-zan-NEE-a).

About 11 million people live in Kenya. About 13 million people live in Tanzania. The capital of Kenya is Nairobi, and the capital of Tanzania is Dar es Salaam.

If you put Kenya and Tanzania together, they would be about as big as Alaska. The area where the Maasai live is about the same size as Indiana.

◀ Some Maasai have moved to cities such as Nairobi.

CHANGING TIMES

Today, it's hard for the Maasai to keep their **traditional** (tra-DI-shun-al) way of life. The laws in their countries make it harder for them to roam with their cattle.

Some Maasai have settled in cities and no longer have cattle. Now, the children go to school, just like you do. The grown-ups work at many different jobs in the towns they live in.

But no matter where the Maasai live, they are still proud to be Maasai.

GLOSSARY

engang (n-GANG) Circle-shaped village where a group of Maasai live.

Kenya (KEN-ya) Country in eastern Africa.

lubega (loo-BAY-ga) Long cotton garment that is worn by all Maasai people.

Maasai (MAH-sigh) Group of people who live in eastern Africa.

mane (MAIN) Hair growing around a lion's face.

Mt. Kilimanjaro (mount kil-i-mon-JA-roe) Highest mountain in Africa.

ocher (OH-kur) Special earth used for body paint.

predator (PRE-da-tor) Wild animal that lives by eating other animals.

savanna (sa-VAN-nah) Flat, wide grassland.

traditional (tra-DI-shun-al) The way a group of people have been doing things for a long time.

Tanzania (tan-zan-NEE-a) Country in eastern Africa.

INDEX